Animal Noses

by Mary Holland

Noses come in all kinds of shapes and sizes. Some are pointed, some are flat. Some are tiny and some are huge. Some are wet and some are dry.

Most noses help animals do two things: breathe and smell. Many animals, like this shrew, use their sense of smell to find food, to find a mate, and to know when danger is near.

Birds do not have a real "nose," but they do have two holes, or nostrils, just above their beak. Can you find a nostril on this young bald eagle? Most birds breathe through their nostrils. Some birds can smell very well, others not so well.

Many animals leave messages for each other by rubbing their scent on a tree or rock, or peeing and pooping in special spots. An animal's scent contains a lot of information.

When another animal of the same kind comes along, it uses its nose to smell the scent and learn who lives there, how old they are, if they are big and strong, if they're looking for a mate, and lots more.

Bears depend on their noses to find a mate and to find food. They rub their backs against trees and leave their scent so that other bears can smell the trees and know who has been there. Black bears can smell food that is several miles away. Grizzly bears can find food under water, and polar bears can smell a seal through three feet (1 m) of ice.

Opossums cannot see or hear very well, but they can smell food from far away. Opossums are not fussy about what they eat. They use their noses to find insects, worms, snakes, frogs, birds, bird eggs, fruits, and mice. Even garbage smells good to an opossum.

White-tailed deer use their noses to find food and to smell predators that might want to eat them. Part of the reason why deer can smell so well is that they keep their noses wet by licking them. Scents stick to wet noses better than dry ones.

Insects don't really have noses. They breathe through tiny holes (spiracles) in their body, and they smell with their antennae. Male moths use their big, feathery antennae to find female moths that are sometimes very far away.

Most snakes can smell better than they can see or hear, but they don't smell with their noses—instead, they use their tongues and mouths. When you see a snake flicking its forked tongue in and out of its mouth, it is smelling something.

The snake collects tiny particles on its tongue and then puts its tongue into two pockets in the roof of its mouth (Jacobson's organ). Then it knows what its tongue has gathered.

Turtles can smell when they are on land and when they are under water. Like snakes, some turtles have a Jacobson's organ which they use to smell.

Frogs use their noses and sense of smell to find mates, to find prey, to keep away from predators, and to find their way home.

Frogs breathe through their noses, but they also breathe through their skin and the inside of their mouth. In order to breathe through their skin, frogs must keep their skin wet.

Some animals have very special noses. A beaver has flaps, or valves, in its nose that act like nose clips. When it dives under water, the flaps close, keeping water out of its nose and allowing the beaver to dive deeper and stay under water longer.

The star-nosed mole gets its name from the shape of its nose. Do you think it looks like a star?

Moles spend a lot of time in their tunnels underground where it is dark and hard to see. They use the 22 little feelers on the tip of their nose to find earthworms and other food to eat.

When a star-nosed mole is looking for food, all the little feelers on its nose wiggle very fast. Can you wiggle your nose very fast like a star-nosed mole?

What is the best thing your nose has ever smelled?

For Creative Minds

Sense of Smell

Everything in the world is made of chemicals. As the air moves, it picks up tiny pieces of everything it touches. It carries these chemicals to your nose.

In the back of your nose is a special patch of skin filled with **chemoreceptors**, also called olfactory receptors. In adults, this area is about the size of a postage stamp.

> *chemo: chemical*
>
> *receptor: a place that takes something in*
>
> A chemoreceptor is a place that takes in chemicals.

When you breathe in through your nose, the air moves through your nose and down into your lungs. The chemicals carried on the wind touch the chemoreceptors at the back of your nose.

The chemoreceptors send a signal to your brain so you know what you are smelling. Most people can sense at least one trillion distinct scents. In general, women are more sensitive to smells than men.

Fun fact: You will probably never have a sense of smell better than you have when you are 8-years old!

Smells

When you have a stuffy nose, you probably can't smell very well—or taste well either! Eighty percent of our taste is related to smell, so when a cold causes nasal obstruction, it not only prevents you from smelling very well, but you also aren't able to taste very much.

Some sicknesses can change the way you smell things. Certain smells may be harder to sense or might smell stronger.

Fun Facts

Bloodhounds have noses ten- to one-hundred-million times more sensitive than a human's.

Bears have a sense of smell seven times stronger than a bloodhound.

Many fish have a well-developed sense of smell.

Albatrosses can find food over 12 miles (19 km) away by smelling it.

Homing pigeons have been shown to use their sense of smell to help find their way home more easily and directly.

Turkey vultures eat mostly decaying bodies of animals which they find by using their sense of smell.

People can detect at least one trillion distinct scents.

Our noses can taste as well as smell. The taste buds on our tongues can only distinguish five qualities: sweet, sour, bitter, salty, and savory (umami). All other 'tastes' are detected by our nose.

black bear

turkey vulture

Match the Nose

Match each animal to its nose:

Striped skunk

Red fox

Eastern chipmunk

Star-nosed mole

A

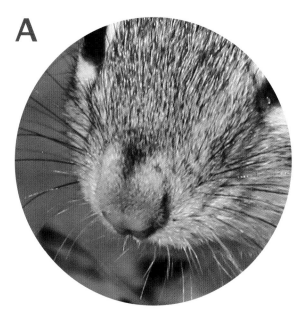

B

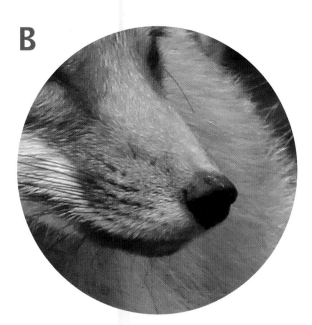

C

D

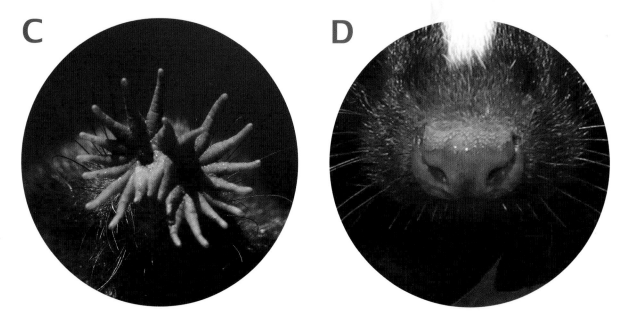

Answers: A: eastern chipmunk. B: red fox. C: star-nosed mole. D: striped skunk

Animals With a Very Good Sense of Smell

Can you guess which of these animals have a good sense of smell?

shark

hairy-tailed mole

luna moth

dog

albatross

Answer: All of them!

All photographs were taken by nature photographer Mary Holland with the exception of the photo of urine in the snow (Susan Holland) and the following photos in the For Creative Minds section: shark (Shutterstock 77472286), dog (Donna German), albatross (Lieutenant Elizabeth Crapo, NOAA Corps)

Thanks to Tia Pinney, Naturalist at Mass Audubon's Drumlin Farm Wildlife Sanctuary in Lincoln, MA for verifying the accuracy of the information in this book.

Library of Congress Cataloging-in-Publication Data

Names: Holland, Mary, 1946- author.
Title: Animal noses / by Mary Holland.
Description: Mt. Pleasant, SC : Arbordale Publishing, [2019] | Audience:
   Grades K-3. | Audience: Ages 4-9. | Includes bibliographical references.
Identifiers: LCCN 2018040510 (print) | LCCN 2018049539 (ebook) | ISBN
   9781607188087 (English PDF) | ISBN 9781643511542 (English ePub) | ISBN
   9781607188100 (Interactive, read-aloud ebook English) | ISBN
   9781607188056 (English hardcover) | ISBN 9781607188063¬(English paperback) | ISBN
9781607188070¬(Spanish paperback) | ISBN 9781607188094¬(Spanish ebook PDF downloadable) | ISBN
9781643513126¬(Spanish ePub) | ISBN 9781607188117¬(Interactive, read-aloud ebook features selectable Spanish)
Subjects: LCSH: Nose--Juvenile literature.
Classification: LCC QL947 (ebook) | LCC QL947 .H65 2019 (print) | DDC
   599.14/4--dc23
LC record available at https://lccn.loc.gov/2018040510

Lexile® Level: 650L
key phrases: animal adaptations

Animals in this book include raccoon (cover), moose (title page), shrew, juvenile bald eagle, red fox, black bear, Virginia opossum, white-tailed deer, Polyphemus moth, garter snake, snapping turtle, spring peeper, beaver, star-nosed mole, child (Otis Brown), porcupine (copyright)

Bibliography/ Bibliografía:

JG-Park Ranger. *Bear Series: Part One A Bear's Sense of Smell.* Yosemite National Park, October 1, 2014. Internet. August, 2018.

Hickman, Pamela M. *Animal senses.* Toronto, Kids Can, 2015.

Holland, Mary. *Naturally Curious: A Photographic Field Guide and Month-By-Month Journey Through the Fields, Woods, and Marshes of New England.* North Pomfret, VT: Trafalgar Square Books, 2010.

Sensory World of Aquatic Organisms, The. Marietta College, January 24, 2002. Internet. August, 2018.

Manufactured in China, December 2018
This product conforms to CPSIA 2008
First Printing

Arbordale Publishing
Mt. Pleasant, SC 29464
www.ArbordalePublishing.com